A GIRL'S A GUN

A GIRL'S A GUN

POEMS

Rachel Danielle Peterson

UNIVERSITY PRESS OF KENTUCKY

Scholarly publisher for the Commonwealth,
serving Bellarmine University, Berea College, Centre
College of Kentucky, Eastern Kentucky University,
The Filson Historical Society, Georgetown College,
Kentucky Historical Society, Kentucky State University,
Morehead State University, Murray State University,
Northern Kentucky University, Transylvania University,
University of Kentucky, University of Louisville,
and Western Kentucky University.
All rights reserved.

Editorial and Sales Offices: The University Press of Kentucky
663 South Limestone Street, Lexington, Kentucky 40508-4008
www.kentuckypress.com

Library of Congress Cataloging-in-Publication Data

Names: Peterson, Rachel Danielle, author.
Title: A girl's a gun : poems / Rachel Danielle Peterson.
Description: Lexington : The University Press of Kentucky, 2017. | Series:
   University Press of Kentucky New Poetry & Prose Series | Includes
   bibliographical references and index.
Identifiers: LCCN 2017042891| ISBN 9780813174433 (pbk. : acid-free paper) |
   ISBN 9780813174440 (pdf) | ISBN 9780813174457 (epub)
Classification: LCC PS3616.E84746 A6 2017 | DDC 811/.6—dc23 LC record
available at https://lccn.loc.gov/2017042891

This book is printed on acid-free paper meeting
the requirements of the American National Standard
for Permanence in Paper for Printed Library Materials.

Manufactured in the United States of America.

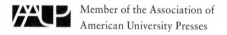

Member of the Association of
American University Presses

For my family:
Katie Beth, Marissa, Sue, Little Bro, Lek & Doc!
And thanks to everyone—
you unnamed multitudes who helped
in great and small ways.
Thanks isn't enough, but it will have to do.

The problems of the human heart in conflict with itself . . . alone can make good writing because only that is worth writing about, worth the agony and the sweat.

—William Faulkner

CONTENTS

Part 1

The Gun

Overlook Kentucky

Dayton, Ohio, 1984

Sie reinigen sich mit Feuer.
"They cleanse themselves with fire."

Sometimes, it turns up ta Mama in polyester,
Those invisibles then or otherwise who kin
read her face, mine. Him, callin' fer Yvonne.

Hey Yvonne! The memoree of some stranger
his shoulder's shadow plunges inta our place:
thunk, thunk. Run! Mother's vowels pierce haze.

Mother, can we distil the pink threads, fabric,
black ball cap, the odor of Bud Light, fills the door
she walks through, dust, Mamma. Dust is all we is

the knock leads inta porch, cement on bare feet,
only a stuffed Bambi knows lips open in prayer
ta a vengeful gawd while another immaculate sun spills

towards another dawn. Somehow, this small pulse
will tense up quite at any doctor too too close ta throat,
toes, all me then blurree, before he gives me paired spectacles.

Whut will linger on, or be charred like barbecue,
tastes I still savor? Wracked on coals, memorees remind us
of shame an' need. Seen, unseen, even gloree can sting.

Journal Entry #1

The Bastard

He knows 'bout his-stor-ee. Say every Thing came outta wahtuh.
Laugh, an . . . Scales? Some maybe. Don't know . . . ask to strip,
show minners low. Decide by those learned men . . . I tol' 'bout
Greeks and glassee sea. Home to Gospel, not desert straws. Told
in Pairee. Home was where we held hands, wishin', 'neath an
ole tree. That rivuh, prongin' hoary roots, cinched like a priest's
hands, those claws. We lived in wahtuh with two heads. Gawds,
jealous of it, cut every-One inta two, maybe ta breed harsh, air
becomes salt in the mouthe, the ache fer sun. Complete—nah. We
jus' long.

Why I Wasn't Supposed to Be Born

Encephalitis it whuz, he caught at Christmas.
They say only miracle can save.

He'll be a vegetable, or dead,
not the best Christmas surprise.

On a loveseat, Maw braids sis's hair inta coils,
a stern gawd, she will glare

as I square, swing, nudge drawers
too loud. I will get born, earn that look,

from the eyes blue as lamp-shade.
They will brighten everything,

I wanna be rough like a beard,
ta hurt mine enemy the way

Paw does, cleave tinsel and IV's the same
as he did on Christmas Day.

This terrible need to know, be known.

Journal Entry #2

Judge

. . . Objective, eye the women eve-va-re wear showing cinched waist. Bared, yessir! Made to milk, as somebody say. Should I docile, open my shirt, counter, whut Gawd needs dugs? Good enough joke. Do ya think true who made such a fuss, made us ta bear, breed out of a squall. Pity-full, full of soul, though, we needs no curve, no linen. Whut then, who, do angels do?

Burn

Just sneak. Smoke with me. Turn upward, imagine billions of star
system, galaxies minute as violet flickerin' at dawn or sunrise.

Beneath us? Fumes from the tip arches there, beyond even this.
Dangerous as fire is, but who can settle when worlds come a
knockin'?

Solid as a door, ya stretch, glimpse long, eye-full 'a solar wind,
The heft of it whispers like a minster's child. Bad is flesh! Bad—!

Yer reply? Ya puff as that cigarette heats against two splayed fin-
gers, measures yer gawddamn mistakes, beyond countin'.

A hair pulls fire from the ash. Ya ain't no dandy-man ta claim ta
know the pure from the stained. Not yer strength, girl.

Breathe, all ya know is this small thing. Lighters, if yer brazen,
will hurt some lips even if ya burn nothin' but the cleanest
    kerosene.

Journal Entry #3

Whut
do ya believe?

Green-blue-gold-flickey iris flayed away 'til mere holy eye flinches
    whole.

Violet, water unknown . . . oh, ripples like twin moles on show-
    der, hidden lights,

fairy-lights in the eye heal wrinkles, scars, life-times, easy as
    coral, pink nail-tips on a kettle,

tea, even stains wash sometime. Or they don't.

New Year's

Back from School

Exhale if ya can in mute Ohio, silent after the scene ends.
It's not hard to praise mist, dappled snow, after fire-works are lit.
Hometowns have churches, communion with wine or grape juice,
Take your pick. I'll take alcohol to see the scene of the angel,
Gabriel, touchin' Our Ladee's knee, not content with just
      whisperin' . . .
Truth now, who didn't creep beneath her arched features in the
      grotto,
Blue-white roses an' thorns, licorice green, just to find somethin'?
Tacky, right? Still, who did I kiss there among hibiscus orange
      obscene?
Confess, yes, the red flew out when I touched it. The bulb.
Someone had left flowers for her. Mary and her electricity.
Why do I feel wrong for not being anything like Mary?
What's a halo but some candle lit to catch sin, hold it in, clean it
      off,
They way ya hold a snowflake in drift with a naked palm.
Who knows, really, but those unknown ages buried now
Dead choirs buried long ago in the cold, cold snow?

Journal Entry #4

When

hands fold in Your Name, who can leave the world un-pressed, sir?

March, still a maid, so I drag breeches, walked with bandy-
        legged, just ta
see, shaved my hair to infatuate bare
nape, ground of bay.

April of Nothings Between, give Glory Many-Named. Sometimes ya
give nuthing back.

May of Vulgar Columbine, candid as a blue corpse, such leave.
Milk-pails are left dry. Sky cleaves her alabaster skirts, ankles
        watery as cloud-burst.

Earth, she speaks in the ache of crickets, heady-musked, like
        lavender, crushed.

I cannot read, but someone reads to me:

Nard and saffron, calamus, cinnamon, incense tree.

. . . I repeat the words, know only three . . .

June of Holy, Holy, Holy
I sing in lace on Sundays, but

bitter Angels keen
See Him
If ya have eyes to see
calamus and incense tree!

Why I Couldn't Marry an Evangelical

He soothes,

> Soon, come, eat clearly.
> Lick a plume blossomin'
> from the tremblin'
> earth, the chains,
> even the vulture's claw.

Journal Entry #5

Do not

touch! Say Jesus in the desert. 'Fore this, all he sought was it.
He was easy, ya see.
so Death's green-eyed angel bent,
curdlin' boulders ta chalk.
While droplets of
some sort could somehow pour over
a sleepin', grievin' Magdalene,
rousin' her from night, those moulderin' tombs,
a veil of sea over there

she'd never, oh never,
contemplate ta cross! No-sir!

Elegy of the Gun

I.

Innocence, Lost

It's the first time, he knows
this already, the man with a belt
against blood-orange Formica,
a true showman at ease, the cop,
gripping the black holster tight.
His sunglasses reflect back at me.

I take it in gleam of steal against steel,
in my pale palm, magic, yer sellin'
some need. Greed is like an itch in my hand.
A twitch, destiny, trains my B-B's site
on the triangular heads. See them all defined?
Salamanders caught in the clear creek water,
brightest before the expulsion.

II.

Speak Easy

I whuz choppin' wood, sir.
Fingernails, coaldust dark, wind about
the clean axe in his grip.
Poppy grins, tells the pigs
he doesn't know, no sir, where those ole
Chicago boys, where they is.
I whuz choppin' in the wood, I believe.

They don't believe, and so they pen him
tight in a checkerboard wagon.
Hooded cops parade him,
my granny's father, past the picket-line,
gray lines form behind. Somebody hoots.
Where's the wood, son?

Martha, his wife, braves every cold,
brings pork loins, custard pie as well.
She heads home later.
Buckshot cascades from a lone car
with windows dim as sin, and holes
start ta convulse above her temple.

III.

Late Arrival

Morning will come late in the mountains,
singin', he's been gone too, too long,
he'll never pay the company back. Nope.
Now, an old elliptic, the will soon bob,
weave above each tree, bright, and necessary as
a miner's headlamp beneath the dirt.

As it swings, it wakes the pent-up bird,
who flexes, rattles steel 'til lulled still
the spell of that false daylight in the shaft.
Out back, a sow nuzzles onions, potato buds,
whatever my father can manage ta forage.
Gawd, he loves that pig, its soft snout.

His small hands extend, divide
while nostrils widen, familiar an' warm.
Dad hears a rifle's click. Goddamn it!
His grandfather's words sharp as a reprimand
as his gun points upward, but the old man's knuckle,
freshly-stitched, hurt from his work.
The mines always hurts someone.

Don't fret. Not in the least, he says
Dad blinks, almost-white as that sow.
Poppy fumbles the old words between them.
Every boy ought ta know, some things,
yessuh, must know something.
The whole world will hurt ya, son!

IV.

Suicide Cliff

A paratrooper, another father, spills,
drips from the womb of an electric sky
born again amid tanks an' airplanes, he stands,
carries the thunder crosswise fer luck
through France, Germany, Japan, but only
Kentucky halts his ascension inta gawd.

The drive is like this weight along his back,
 the parachute he wore as he dove,
when they said son, yer far from home,
long before bombs, their shell of eyes,

sullied his memories. The dead and the living,
he's found, are just the same in this light.

Only the Lawd is great, quite enough,
whut the milk-faced preacher said
pointin' at the ceiling, the church's mural
of a penciled, circular sky. Heaven fer
you an' I. Just you an I. All ya needs do is die.
Seemed right, ta him. Back home, it seems alright

ta hold the ole war rifle like a crucifix,
it kept him from fallin' too hard off the track.
It seems good ta forget as it can,
the bleak black fields of France.
The muzzle, so sleek, small, can make one forget
fear, everything, make one feel like gawd must feel.

Mother sees the rifle, so dark against his temple.
Bleary-eyed, he will tongue arsenic, to fly again.
A terrible fit foams up Holy Spirit on his tongue,
When the sirens serenade, he's prepared his speech.
He knows it by heart, clear as sunlight
bright against his skin, he knows it all. Every word!

V.

Palm Reader

In Florida, someone walks ta her bed
gropes fer a Nerf toy Sis musta hid beneath her pink quilt.

He feels something stick there as he squints
at it, the red mucks tainin' his fingers, loafers, every part.
Later, they find him still there, her blood minglin'
wiped across one singular cheek.

In the swamp, his parents tape the killer's picture
to an old willow tree, offer their son all they have
ta give him, a black B-B gun an' ammo.
They want him whole, so they say, it'll be alright, son.
Pat his back. Over the hill, he will toss it aside
only when it is flimsy, empty, as his eyes were then.

My balding cousin was tried fer it, died in Texas
by lethal injection, some steel-haired governor's decree
as he inclined his Stetson on *Hard Copy,* drawled on
how serial killers need to be erased from history.
Mama aimed a finger at the screen we watched,
He whuz so quiet, like the real world whuz just inside him.

The only time she said anything ta me.
Shiverin', I couldn't help it, as I read the book about him.
The gray mugshot on the cover had bright, even teeth,
dark hair doggin' the white, upper lip.
In flaring font below, it said, COULD HAPPEN ANYTIME!
That is true enough. More than true, I think.

A young girl alone lets him inside. She couldn't help it,
but be polite as she was taught. He's charmed. It's not his first
      time.

He shows it quick, for he knows metal is best inscribed with
    shiverin'.
Oh you wretched thing, turn yer mild eye away,
The rest, we must know that his heart is nothin' but hollow bone,
a gun, ready ta pop, explode over someone because it is love ta
    him.

He runs the gun along her cheek's hollow, draws his thumbs
    along
her windpipe, prefers the blush of maid, her virgin charm,
pale skin then sudden red when he will break her in, like a gawd,
the Roman one, another Hymen. In Miami, the freckled boy,
her brother, won't ever sleep without a knife beneath his pillow.
He'll don sunglasses, learn ta interrogate an' hold a rifle right,
    yessir.

VI.

Fire-Bringer

In Dayton, will I dream or wake up ta find
the same, slick tang of tongue, salamanders that skulk about
with war in their eye as they rise? Bright esophagi
spurt plumes, geysers that churn all creek, continental divides.
Except inside, not at this heart-hollow, nope.
Lower, some Old Defiant will somehow clutch my belly

with fingers so cool with precision. He'll seize my neck,
arch against me, make me greet his face,
tender as a slitherin' fist inta teeth. You know the rest of the story.

Muses get fuckin' burned like witches, bad girls
who wear the wrong thing to church or the grocery store
or at home. All girls are bad to someone, even me.

I shot them dead, yet I see, always see them still in the water,
neither dead nor livin', but risin' up like new suns:
muscular lime with dark veins, mottled black,
dots of orange an' cream, rusted auburn with sable acne,
the blue-spotted, rouge-templed, burgundy.
The beautiful tragedy I see it all. Yes, I see them burn out the sky!

Love Is the Battlefield

Always the swords   empty stomach.

Women in Hebron   lilt

coquette,   soon made

of stone.   Soldiers, fist,

deep tongues   from maiden, crone

squeal shrill, dumb   as any pig.

Dark-eyed mammas   knived

sons, girls   to pray, always

as she hove   spatula, grievous

our Prophet.   We'll remind 'em,

Charity, yessah   manna

from words   chemical. Oh

moan from stone   can she

sometime   come home

can she feed me?

A Wish to Die

I jumped, yeah, at some point, ta escape,
Fine word as any ta a caught bird wantin' free.
We all do at times 'cause "safety" is another net
An' I ain't ever been *that*. Can ya count on all
Fingers an' toes each sigh, each, every time I try,
Ta ring like a struck bell's *lulay*. Go on, try it out.
Give up eatin' fer days on Holy Week, tempt Gawd
On yer knees. He is a god, a man. He just might try.
Ya seem stuck on him an', well, everybody ta look.
Well, don't huff if all ya get is an empty ache.
That's holiness, yep. We die every-time from it,
Too much need, fire or whiskey, or bullies ya leave
Dyin' cold in a long, narrow street. Might as well
Return after each—even if ya ain't done yet, not in the least.

Part 2

The Girl

Soldier of God

First arc
toward Gawd.

>   *Is he dead . . .*

More than me.

>   *You faked your wounds there.*

Yessuh.

>   *What will happen if they have*
>   *no use for you?*

Then God will
make use a' me.

>   *Would you marry?*

Well, If it whuz
His ider.

>   *You'd stop being The Maid? How will*
>   *you know?*

I know. Then the doing.
If I mistake, then I will ask recompense.

Aren't you scared?

Ev'body skeer'd.
Ya just need enough love ta drive it off.

Scared of you?

Don't cha fear?

Always.

Whut, then?

Losing.

We'll neva lose. The Lawd is with us.

I mean, losing you.

I'm a country girl. I think ya've
recovered from several, right?

(His hand slants my chin.)

This will is not my own.
Fear Hell, if you fear not Gawd.

Perhaps your God sent me.

So alone,
so soft beneath

armor, as if
it never wore you.

No,
don't sing to me.
I've heard it.

> *No one can see*
> *Feel your softness*
> *There, feel that*
> *You can be soft too*

From behind
a growl,
a torn hem,
is this what I came for?
yes, take slit me

yes *o*	*this hard?*
sweet miseries	*o sweet o*
God in me	*I come*
then gone.	*god, feel me . . . can you*

Harlan County

Home is in the vocal chords—
the sound. Lost now, as the tune.
My murmur slips up to mother's room,
my first one here in Harlan County.

In the same hospital, the same headboard
my mother and I fell into florescent lights,
while the same blood reddened the same linoleum,
maybe mere "coincidence" in Harlan County.

Black Mountain, named after coal,
the thick, fern-fingered ridges that show
my first birdsong, yellow finches,
in the cradle-space of Harlan County.

My father did whistle as he threaded
hope into veins of grim, glittering earth
until the ridgepoles lay stripped like
naked thighs can be in Harlan County.

We left the rock, the redbud's soil
that stained his fingers for where the
glacier flattened Ohio, but kept the Word,
in the steep syllables of Harlan County.

I level my mother-tongue on highways,
clip every consonant, while father,
street-maker, story-shaper, still
bloodies the sun for Harlan County.

The One

I was cursed with eyes of emerald, to leave
the backdoor unlocked, and he would see
would fill the room, such a head of honey-hue,
more blonde than most I've found.
Amid acres of soybeans lush, strange,
like he always was, like I could be,
I was Dorthy to his Cheshire King.
He ran, shirtless, through fields.
He had a smile without a cat.
It would spread from him to me,
from one kiss from the red tenderness of lips.
One breath, and you'd disappear, you'd die.
Dangerous predicament for those without soul.
Though different in many ways, there was little
I held back, wouldn't let him slip in,
a cancer stick shared between the meeting
of our eyes. I felt responsible, do it right,
for goddamn once. But, always there are always but's.
Sometimes, there was grass in his mouth,
and his face held a look like brass,
cattish, inward. One pregnancy scare made him
Existential to cross his emptiness,
fear of death. No human could comfort him,
no matter how he'd worship a knee.
At the back door with some SoCo, he said,
write but don't write about me, so I didn't,
I tried to do it right, and write about
Odysseus, another sharp one. Didn't you know

that he could dive like a shark?
Like him, I have few fears now
because I've been beneath clothes,
beneath water, until a part of me was gone.
He loved the crush of ocean in his ear,
like I love the reach of the sea.
Even if he forgot my smell, I recollect
the aroma of Old Spice, bourbon whiskey
as clear as anything can be. How I wish,
why do always wish for what will never be?

Saint Joan

When you kill like Joan
descend shield

before the man, mace
shatters brain-cage.

The foam, drips, hides
the grin of statecraft accompli.

Sword snorts buckler
like fish dumbstruck by air, so

elemental, the clank,
likely to blade, snarl gross.

only the screw,
sinew along sinew.

Entomb a Buck Knife
in Adam's Apple. Don't believe

in how the blood spurts
ragged, a crescendo of groan,

like fumes, incense flung
from a censer.

Spilled, the godly cries out

Deliverance, but you sink

into the nearest stream,
bellow for any medicine,

waterskin to remove the weight,
dead, torsos, meat, men.

Then thunder, rain, crashes down.
You try to breathe, but scream loud,

Oh God, to be free
across the goddam sea!

For Another Dancer

Janis, the edge can be slippery.
We have both fallen from dreams we made.
Dreams are overdone, set them free tonight.
Did you have a Mamma like me, always behind ya?
Mother, dead for so long, appears sparkly,
Smelling of Vidal Sassoon and Dial.

Mother is but a dream we sell each other
Over a Friendly's vanilla ice cream sundae.
You only appear then in the booth. Wail,
The way I want to be loosened within.
When my lips move, Mamma says ta shove it,
Finger hard at lips, hard as her love.

Can I ever be loved?

Birthday

March 2012

Not for him

He dresses, eyes again
the suitcase, bill, while
coatracks glimmer
excuses always gleam.
The keyring loosens doors
faces only glimpsed
in a photo, the wallet
he'll never show.
I imagine, yes, with
all of my inadequacies,
white as cheap hotel sheets.
They're all cheap.
Nothing can buy
The bruises on each knee,
tell them how
you laugh at him,
you, love like you knew.
Flick it away,
withdraw the things
you wrap your self in,
the jut of wrists,
shame and reprimands.
The heart is cruel,
an organ with no song.
We make it all up

to understand why
the best of me, my baby
was there, and then gone.
The red radio played on,
but bodies tell, Chicago,
they nail us to cartography:
brute as hips, empty seas.

A Memorial of a Memorial

Candles held in hands as if floating over a river of darkness,
they halt as if waiting for gold, illumination.

What can I tell them? Waves and rain remind me of dead ancestors.
Memories are our mirror.

The brine, water touches sky, do you remember what a cloud is?
Who knows why we swim and swim and swim . . .

Love Song of the Sea-Girl

In the rearview mirror:
        passenger's side,
           marine eyes, patina.
Sweat. Just you and me
in a hushed, hothouse flush.

Scrape and save,
        just scrap the sulk
        of holy here.
No priest to crook my knee,
say naughty. Naughty!

Feel the god within me
        flee somewhere low,
        like a
hanged man's soul
flees where? We don't know.

Lover, you smile
        that solid grin
        from braces and bleach,
sign a heart on
each beaded windowpane.

I should just shush,
        be sweetie pie, dove,
        beneath the dread

lull, the hymn, the
windshield's swift wipe.

Catastrophe can be fine
        sometimes, when found
        in a catapult, words
from a slur.
I won't get hurt again.

I'll leave, caress the steel,
        the wheel that bends
        this way, neither
a king nor prince of anything,
just a trim-coifed queen alone.

Cleopatra and her billions,
        those stony-eyed few,
        mermen so swoony,
they still crave
a tune about *then*.

I'll give them a song.
        Way down in Egypt's land,
        I grow up. I grow up.
O Lordy, let my people do the same,
but they will never grow up.

So, I will watch
        the Derby and sip
        a mint julep, elegant

and be forgot.
You'll enter from behind.

My gods, still my eyes,
        extend us beneath
        that delicate shell.
Any moon is made of honey,
if you hold fast, tight,

when you open my mouth,
        red as a gill
        or a wound,
I'll croon for you, sweet baby,
Only you.

His-story Lessons

They say that "You'll Never Leave Harlan Alive," but God told
    me, so I must,
Sore as need, I slipped away, became Apollo, Artemis, sometime,
    in deed.

Thought only gets you so far. I learned well to intuit passion from
    prison cells, the release.
Fer me and mine, at least. You don't need Johnny Cash to tell ya,
    friends, we all die

In our beds or desks or maybe outside. Why mate death then, the
    decline?
Day or night's just fine by me. Sweet mountain laurel sticks to my
    molars anywho.

You will get all bedecked with trumpery. What we always name
    our first tongue trophy,
Find it in the sea, the damn honeysuckle plucked as I hankered
    for more, yes, more!

Greedy I will be, I is, even when I become old. Mother, dead but
    still alive to me,
Will their lips be moist enough to kiss? Caged, locked, who will it
    be, who will they see,

Who will loosen every nicety? You, or god, or me—no—I—I
    must climb it,

The ladder toward love, love, love so high, defy every eye here,
    there, wise-like.

We can, I think. You like finality. Tonight or Tuesday, look on the
    stilted, jilted rock we press
Up against, toward . . . Whatever she's done, she left Harlan alive.
    Have you left yet?

Canopy

When I lean down toward earth, set me face in it, you know that
    is when you appear
        the tang of elbows on stone.
I have never been afraid to be with the dead of cemeteries. I
    would be there sometimes
        a hand reaching along a thigh.
Now, I have reason enough to fear the dead, those ghosts of the
    men and women who
        made me, the ones I will know,
No matter how many times I break against the brute waves, I will
    be open inside, and
        the edged canopy will bend down,
A fetish of some supernatural tribe to summon the god-demon or
    god-child, nearest to water
        to face the sea inside,
The hardest thing. I'm no good. You know that I will meet each
    god with a snarl that mirrors theirs,
        the same stiff shuffle.
Maple leaves and the autumnal lure of sap and syrup drawn out
    of brittle bark, the old
        miracles are known again,
Tremble all you appearances and gestures of greater purposes
    than I can ever fathom,
        you don't exist, never existed!
I can move and be both separate and connected, the way a cloud
    disappears at night
        into the infinite black canopy—yes!
Always moving toward something else . . .

The Morrigan

Sell my despair? Don't dally
head nor heart.
Oh Hero, keep your holies!

Grails are legends, hard
to drink from every day.

Halo and poinsettia,
bloody spikes,
purchase my place.

Even I deserve rest,
everlasting cups.

Woe to the mossy,
bolted rock,
you cling to instead.

Ruts are rudimentary,
love is much, much harder.

Just don't go,
don't leave,
without me. You will though!

Lust is dust.
I dream of it,

dream of love,
a verdant, slow, low honey-color
I'll keep

tender, before it's
too painful to know.

Feel me
worlds away.
Can you not,

the long, hot skin, coconut
or eel? Hard to say, folks.

Branches, for some,
swing beneath
long, moist tongues

with such flame
in red flourish, bud.

Always will follow
like a dog,
wet or dry, words spoke

that night of enameled sky.
No more sighs,

Never again, Lord.

He is DEAD,
dead to me

like the so arched,
brim, world, my love

All I see
is white.
All dies, keep the

orchestral low, silent.
That adds a bit more space.

There is no
dreadful sip
of honey, no color, no,

nothing worth the honor,
eloquent speech tonight,

only nails,
nails there—
dark and sharp

in the laundry bin.

Kill the Beast

If Beauty married the Beast . . .

Where
        did it go, Father?
        They've shaved

it, my head,
        Dark, lavish.

Cut it,
        you'll only
        see it return.

Make it
        a man again.
        I do it

to end you.
        A Cain,
        I was made

to spite ya.
        in death.
        Here, my soul

is useful twine,
easy to part
        as Moses,

he who flew
>> into blue.
>> Every shade

becomes his, yessir.
>> Can you be
>> too too heavy

with soul?
>> Come loosen
>> all yer gods,

I know,
>> you know,
>> the rope

makes us
>> afraid
>> to change.

Rivulets
>> spite you,
>> cry out,

hold thunder,
>> these tears.
>> Here,

The Maid!
>> The Light inside
>> washes

hard as Hell.
      Hail
      Fathers to

yer woundin',
      true son.
      Mama, tell,

the heart
      beats the thrum,
      of war-drum!

GOD SO GORY,
      GIRL only GLORY!
      Hope is come.

Such
      a violent thing,
      love,

brief
      as gray,
      insistent waves,

the creek
      murmurs
      like dead shoulders,

drowning

ferns
and boulders,

and

no man
escapes
her

I want
ta see
her

Redbird

for Sarah Hubbs

"If happiness never comes, what is a life?"

July 2015, Saipan

When you live in Ohio, you live for oxygen,
even the girl who was shot in her mouth
in her bedroom on a very clear day.
Ohio was hard on us, but I will always survive,
take more than I need, yessir, wrap my legs
around something, even as they hush me.

∾

Boom, that's what tragedy feels
Like you can never return again.

∾

Even if you've lost your eyes,
I will tell you wonders that will drip
lifeblood onto lashes,
Even if you can't hear me,
does it matter?

∾

I wasn't as good a friend
As I should be, never am.

Sometimes, I am afraid that I
Don't need people enough.

Sometimes, maybe, too much.
I tell myself a lie older than any cemetery.

Lean close, maybe I'll tell you.
Only the dead should hear it,

Maybe you're dead—or will be.
The page you touch now,

the sly soul that fills in
when dense eye strays down.

You want a good story.
So, I'll have ta improvise:

Imagine this—

jagged outlines, molten galaxies
coal and volcano, we have tears that beat
the brain an' heart, the inevitable groans.
Their need? Ta crack open, like a comet's flame,
a tangled hand down into black hair,
gray or blue—none of it matters then!
the flare of the sun, one constellation,
Three Fingers that spark the darkness.

        ∾

So, let the suns explode,
But will my lover come

Dripping honey?
The question you dead can't ask,

but I can. I have to.

∾

Cardinals do,
but who can truly
mate for life?

No one
that I have
clenched mid-flight.

Can birds
be truer
than we suppose?

O plumes
of gray-blue,
crimson-hue we'll have.

Yes, I'll lose
myself,
and have to wing it.

The cardinals
will somehow
gore, scatter the

glistening
seedpods of
these graves,

their flowers,

hibiscus, and—God—
red-violet leaves

falling in
an April shower,
another flaming tree,

not just
in Kentucky,
but everywhere,

something red
will break out.
Sweet honey

on the rock,
that's what they say
on the day

the past can be revised.

Here's my attempt, anyway:

Around 2005, the porch-light flickered off, then on. He blocked
      the doorway with a human outline, a shadow.
Either, we stumbled toward the falls. The wallop grazed each
    eardrum.
        Wading in calf-deep, I was happy, strong, splashed him
wanting to peel off my clothes, the water to whir like a prism
      hiding every distraction. I wanted to be hip-deep,

in you and me, at you, at us, before inevitability.

Close your eyes, feel this lay on your forehead. Tell me
        again about the faucet, water Mama drew so hot
that the porcelain wept deep as anguish.
        Hard to tell. Maybe the wet came from over there,
your lashes hesitating to give way, to flutter.
        Either way, you bit that pouting bottom lip,
groaning all the while for the content you get
        from lipstick on nose's cradle, you don't
wanna rub it off. Just like I am made to hunger
        after the musk of your dark, hidden hairs,
trilling for each and all. Even you, marked by
        freckles, scars, divides, be proud of each,
these kisses savored under sun, yes,
        the sun inside, and someday right now
my fragrant, flowered love. By some magic bullet
        or by sunshine, some way, every page will rise
into sky, like oxygen, from those red lips to mine

ACKNOWLEDGMENTS

Many thanks to the editors of the publications in which several of these poems first appeared, sometimes in slightly different forms.

"Harlan County" originally appeared in the Chicago-based journal *Arsenic Lobster* 30 (Winter 2012). The poem was also published in the April 2017 edition of *Front Porch Journal,* the literary journal of Texas State University's MFA program.

Cleft of Sky was a semifinalist for the 2013 Trio House Press Award for a First/Second Book, which was judged by Mihaela Moscaliuc, and it was selected as an honorable mention for the 2014 Joanna Cargill Coconut Book Prize for a First Book.

"Elegy of the Gun," which was originally published by the *Los Angeles Review* (March 2013), was nominated for Best New Poets 2013. "Elegy of the Gun: V" was on display in the Poetry Leaves Exhibition, May 2–31, 2017, and published in *Poetry Leaves, Volume 2,* both of which were sponsored by the Waterford Township Public Library in Ann Arbor, Michigan.

"Saint Joan" was originally published in the Paris-based journal *Her Royal Majesty* 13 (Summer 2013).

"New Year's" was nominated for Best New Poets 2014 by Ashland University.

"Redbird" was originally published in *The Burden of Light: Poems on Illness and Loss,* edited by Tanya Chernov. "Redbird" was nominated for Best New Poets 2014 by Ashland University.

"Why I Wasn't Supposed to Be Born" was originally published in *Revolver* (March 21, 2014), which is sponsored by a literary arts organization based in Lowertown, St. Paul, Minnesota.

NOTES

The epigraph is from William Faulkner's speech at the Nobel Banquet at Stockholm City Hall, December 10, 1950.

A Girl's A Gun takes its title from an Australian band of the same name. This name was inspired by the famous quote from several sources, and René Clair also used it in a speech on the art of cinema delivered in Geneva in 1967: "The public's tastes change but what attracts it most often is what our master D. W. Griffith defined thus, more than forty years ago: 'A girl and a gun,' that is, eroticism and violence." The title was also strongly inspired by the songs "Me and a Gun" by Tori Amos and "Dog Days are Over" by Florence and the Machine.

"Overlook Kentucky" is dedicated to the German poet Rainer Maria Rilke. The quote is not from his work but rather a German phrase, *"Sie reinigen sich mit Feuer,"* which roughly means "They clean themselves with fire" or "They clean themselves using fire."

"New Year's" is inspired by Hamlet's first monologue in Shakespeare's *Hamlet.*

"Elegy of the Gun" was inspired by a certain Emily Dickinson poem as well as an article about my cousin Lee Burgan, a serial killer who was executed in Texas for killing a police officer. The article profiled the brother of one of Burgan's victims, who went on to become a police officer. Section I from "Elegy of the Gun" ("Innocence, Lost") takes its title from John Milton's *Paradise Lost,* an epic poem about the fall of man. Section II ("Speak Easy") takes its title from the Prohibition-era term for a bar, and the events described in section II take place in the 1920s. Section III ("Late Arrival") takes its name from the practice of reserving a room for a late guest on the condition that if said guest fails to arrive, he or she is held liable for a fee. Section IV ("Suicide Cliff") takes its name from Laderan Banadero, a cliff near San Roque, Saipan, in the Northern –Mariana Islands. Many Japanese soldiers and civilians leaped from the cliff after the Japanese were defeated by American forces at the Battle of Saipan. Section V ("Palm Reader") takes its name from "palm reading," also referred to as *palmistry* or *chiromancy*, in which one's future is supposed to be predicted by interpreting the meaning of the lines on his or her hand. Section VI ("Fire Bringer") takes its name from Prometheus, a Titan who defied the gods to bring fire to humankind as recounted in Greek mythology. The etymology of Prometheus's name is hotly debated. Some claim it is derived from the proto-Indo-European root of the Vedic *pra math,* i.e., "to steal," hence *pramathyu*-s or "thief," cognate with "Prometheus," who stole fire. A Vedic myth describes Mātariśvan, who has much in common with the Greek Prometheus. The main difference was *pramantha,* the Vedic term for the tool first used to create fire.

"Saint Joan" is about Joan of Arc (Jeanne d'Arc), the only saint who was executed by the Catholic Church yet canonized hundreds of years later. There are many depictions of Joan, including some that date from her lifetime, but modern scholars point to her resemblance to conquerors such as Alexander the Great.

"For Another Dancer" is dedicated to Janis Joplin. The other artist mentioned is Aerosmith and their song "Janie's Got a Gun." I have set it to music.

"Love Song of the Sea-Girl" is my re-imagining of T. S. Eliot's "The Love Song of J. Alfred Prufrock."

"His-story Lessons" refers to the song "You'll Never Leave Harlan Alive."

"The Morrigan" is titled after the ambiguous Irish goddess of the same name, who seems to represent both death and life.

"Kill the Beast" takes its title from a song in Walt Disney's *Beauty and the Beast.* "Le Pont Mirabeau" by Guillaume Apollinaire was another inspiration.

The poem "Redbird" is dedicated to Sarah Hubbs, a childhood friend who passed away before this manuscript was completed. A line from Edith Södergran's "A Life," translated from the Swedish by Averill Curdy, begins the poem. The girl who was shot refers to a gunshot victim who was found in her bedroom in Huber Heights, Ohio. The poem itself was inspired by several sources. The cardinal is the state bird of Ohio. One Cherokee myth relates how the redbird was the daughter of the sun, and there is a persistent superstition that seeing a cardinal is a sign of good luck. The mythical phoenix in China is often tied to the dragon, and they are depicted either as mortal enemies or as blissful lovers.

THE UNIVERSITY PRESS OF KENTUCKY
NEW POETRY AND PROSE SERIES

This series features books of contemporary poetry and fiction that exhibit a profound attention to language, strong imagination, formal inventiveness, and awareness of one's literary roots.

SERIES EDITOR: Lisa Williams

ADVISORY BOARD: Camille Dungy, Rebecca Morgan Frank, Silas House, Davis McCombs, and Roger Reeves

Sponsored by Centre College

CPSIA information can be obtained
at www.ICGtesting.com
Printed in the USA
BVOW09s0744290917
496025BV00001B/2/P